All About Us

Written and Illustrated by

Ethel Sinofsky

Credits:
Written and Illustrated by Ethel Sinofsky
Book Design by David G. O'Neil

Published by
Story Trust Publishing, LLC
36 Floral Street
Newton, Massachusetts 02461
www.storytrust.com

Printed in the United States of America

Paperback Edition
ISBN: 978-1-937228-03-3

Dedication

For my great-grandchildren,
named here in alphabetical order:
Abby
Carina
Elijah
Emily
Julia
Kailey
Kalman
Kayla
Keely
Rachel
Sarah
Sydney
and "Yet To Have A Name"

Acknowledgements

My thanks to my nearest and dearest who encouraged my efforts, made thoughtful suggestions, and applauded my small successes.

And my grateful thanks to my friend and mentor, David O'Neil, without whom this book would never have seen the light of day. He told me I could do this, and then proceeded to encourage, help, prod, and push me—to prove to me that, indeed, I could!

We have a HEAD and 2 FEET,

and 10 FINGERS and 10 TOES,

and 2 EARS and 1 CHIN,

and EYES to open or close.

We have TEETH and a TONGUE,

so we can eat and we can talk.

And our 2 LEGS can move,

so we can run and can walk.

When we sit, we have a LAP,

but
<u>not</u>
when
we
stand!

And at the end of each ARM

there is a
LEFT or RIGHT
HAND.

Our mouth has 2 LIPS,

and what is nice about this is,
that while our arms give a hug
our LIPS can give kisses.

I almost forgot about NOSES,
that sometimes run and can sneeze,

but they let you smell roses,
and fresh, rain-washed leaves.

And did I mention our ELBOWS,
our ANKLES and KNEES?
Do you know how many we each have of these?

We have SHOULDERS and WRISTS,
and a FRONT and a BACK.
We have so many parts
that it's hard to keep track!

and a TUMMY that shakes,

and HIPS that can WIGGLE!

We've a BRAIN that's our body's computer,
sending messages to our every part,
so we SPEAK, or MOVE, or LEARN new things.

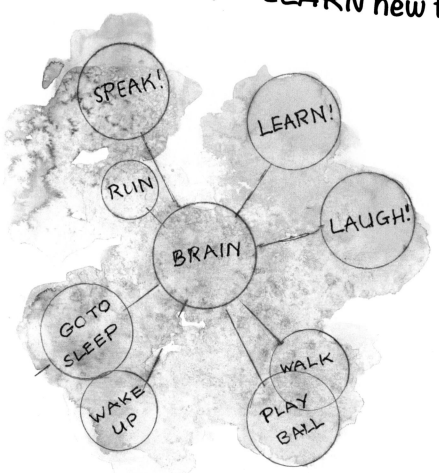

It's the BRAIN that makes us smart!

And with our VOICE we can speak about our FEELINGS, or say

"PLEASE" and

"THANK YOU," or

"HAVE A NICE DAY!"

And FEELINGS are something
you can't often see,

but we have lots of them, always,
not just two or three.

We have feelings of LOVE
and sometimes of SADNESS,

of ANGER, of FRIENDSHIP,
and of HOPE and of GLADNESS.

And we've a HEART really small

that beats in our CHEST,

and when that's filled with LOVE

is when we feel the BEST!

To order copies of *All About Us*,
please visit www.storytrust.com.

Story Trust®

Story Trust Publishing, LLC
storytrust.com

Made in the USA
Coppell, TX
02 March 2021

51103123R00017